Flowchart Smart

THE SCIENCE OF DESERTS

Richard and Louise Spilsbury

Gareth Stevens PUBLISHING

Please visit our website, **www.garethstevens.com**.
For a free color catalog of all our high-quality books,
call toll free 1-800-542-2595 or fax 1-877-542-2596.

Cataloging-in-Publication Data

Names: Spilsbury, Richard. | Spilsbury, Louise.
Title: Deserts / Richard and Louise Spilsbury.
Description: New York : Gareth Stevens Publishing, 2020. | Series: Flowchart smart | Includes glossary and index.
Identifiers: ISBN 9781538252215 (pbk.) | ISBN 9781538252192 (library bound)
Subjects: LCSH: Deserts--Juvenile literature. | Desert ecology--Juvenile literature.
Classification: LCC GB612.S65 2020 | DDC 551.41'5--dc23

First Edition

Published in 2020 by
Gareth Stevens Publishing
111 East 14th Street, Suite 349
New York, NY 10003

Produced for Gareth Stevens by Calcium
Editors: Sarah Eason and Harriet McGregor
Designer: Emma DeBanks
Picture researcher: Rachel Blount

Picture credits: Cover: Shutterstock: Macrovector (br), YummyBuum (c); Inside: Shutterstock: Asharkyu: p. 13r; Larry Barrett: pp. 24-25; Baseart: p. 19t; Bufo: p. 11t; Christian_b: pp. 32-33; MB Creative: p. 43c; Wojciech Dziadosz: p. 7t; Max Earey: p. 5t; EcoPrint: pp. 28-29; Eivaisla: p. 33br; Anton Foltin: pp. 12-13; Giuseppe_R: p. 30; Ken Griffiths: pp. 18-19; IrinaK: p. 17r; Lady-luck: p. 23; Pranesh Luckan: pp. 16-17; Janelle Lugge: p. 21c; MarcvanKessel.com: pp. 6-7; Martha Marks: p. 37t; Tim Murphy: pp. 44-45; NadyaEugene: pp. 40-41; NaniP: pp.26-27; Nattanan726: pp. 20-21; Nepart: pp. 38-39; Alice Nerr: p. 45b; Pan_photo: p. 41t; Charles T. Peden: pp. 34b, 34-35; Anton Petrus: pp. 4-5; Ray Redstone: pp .10-11; Smit Saengchot: p. 43c (bg); Stefan Scharf: p. 26b; Alexey Stiop: pp. 36-37; Theron Stripling III: pp. 1, 29b; Vectorlight: p. 8c; VectorShow: p. 9; VeronikaMaskova: p. 14; Wildpix productions: p. 24b.

Printed in the United States of America

CPSIA compliance information: Batch #CW20GS: For further information contact Gareth Stevens, New York, New York at 1-800-542-2595.

Contents

Chapter 1

What Are Deserts?

Deserts cover about one-fifth of Earth's entire land surface. They are some of the harshest and most challenging **ecosystems** on our planet.

The most significant nonliving feature of a desert ecosystem is the lack of water. Deserts are areas of land that are **arid** and receive fewer than 10 inches (25 cm) of rain, snow, or other **precipitation** each year. In some deserts, there is no rainfall for months or years at a time. Others get regular but light rains that add up to very little water over an entire year. Deserts are dry because they are in places with very hot or very cold **climates**. Many deserts are scorching hot during the day but the temperature drops to freezing at night.

An ecosystem is made up of all of the living and nonliving things that **interact** with one another in an area. It includes living things, such as plants and animals, and nonliving things, such as the weather, sunlight, and soil. All ecosystems have their own features. The desert ecosystem includes everything in the desert, from tiny grains of sand to large desert animals.

The Arabian oryx's light color reflects heat and sunlight, so this horned antelope can surive extreme desert temperatures.

Deserts such as the Sahara are covered in hills of sand, piled up by the wind. These are sand dunes.

Get Smart!

There are deserts scattered across the globe. The biggest deserts in the world are the freezing Antarctic and Arctic deserts at the South and North **Poles**. The largest hot desert on Earth is the Sahara Desert. It occupies most of North Africa.

Types of Deserts

All deserts are dry, but different types of deserts form in different ways depending on where they are located.

A rain shadow desert forms on one side of a tall mountain range. When wind blows toward the mountain, it is forced up the steep side of the slope. As the air rises, it cools and **condenses**. The **water vapor** in it turns from a gas into liquid water and falls as heavy rain. By the time the air reaches the far side of the mountain it is dry. With little or no rainfall in the area, a desert forms. Death Valley in the United States is a rain shadow desert.

The Atacama Desert in Chile formed in the rain shadow of the Andes Mountains. It is also a coastal desert.

Get Smart!

Some deserts form at coasts that run along a cold ocean. When cold winds blow air over the coast, the water vapor in the air condenses and forms a fog. If the water droplets in this fog are too small and light to fall from the sky as rain, they can **evaporate** in the hot daytime sun instead.

Polar deserts form where the air is very cold. Earth's polar deserts are found in the Arctic and Antarctic. The air rarely becomes warm enough for the water vapor within it to fall as rain. When any precipitation does fall from the sky, it falls as snow. When it lands on the cold surface below, it never melts. Polar deserts are permanently covered in vast, flat layers of ice. It is also dark for months every year, so few living things can survive there.

More than 98 percent of Antarctica is covered with ice. There is almost no liquid freshwater at all, making Antarctica the driest desert of all.

Get flowchart smart!

How Rain Shadow Deserts Form

Let's find out how rain shadow deserts form.

Rain shadow deserts form on one side of a mountain range, away from the wind.

By the time the air reaches the far side of the mountain, it is dry.

With little or no rainfall in the area, a desert forms.

When wind blows toward the mountain, it is forced up the side of the mountain.

As the air rises, it cools and condenses.

The water vapor in the air turns from a gas into a liquid, and falls as rain.

Flowchart Smart

Chapter 2

Desert Plants

All living things need water to survive, but desert plants have adapted to live without water for extended periods of time.

The biggest and most famous desert plants are cacti. Cactus stems have folds or pleats that expand to store water after rain has fallen. They shrink again as the water is used up. Saguaro cacti are the tallest of all. They have one very long deep root that holds them in the ground. Other, smaller roots grow just below the surface so they can quickly absorb any rain that falls on the land. These roots spread out over a wide area to soak up as much water as they can and the saguaro's stem expands to store it all.

Saguaro cacti can grow as tall as a four-story house and live for 200 years. They grow in deserts in the southwestern United States and Mexico.

The creosote bush has small, pointed green leaves with a waxy coating. The waxy leaves prevent the plant from losing water and help it survive high temperatures. The plant can live for more than two years with no water at all, by dropping its leaves and even some of its branches. The creosote bush also grows new plants from shoots at the top of its roots, which spread out to cover a wide area. This ensures no other plants can grow near it. It therefore gets to keep all the rain that falls nearby for itself. Creosote bushes are so well adapted for desert life that they can live for hundreds of years.

Many desert animals, such as kangaroo rats and other rodents, dig burrows among the roots beneath a well-established creosote bush.

Get Smart!

In a desert, water is hard to find. Many animals would like to eat cactus stems to get the water stored inside them. Cactus plants' leaves have adapted to become hard spikes. This keeps thirsty animals from being able to eat them.

Plant Life Cycles

Some plants survive in the desert by growing and dying back in one short season, before the weather becomes too hot and dry.

When rain falls in the desert, some flowering plants immediately start to grow. Seeds that have been dormant, or resting, beneath the surface begin to grow into plants. They quickly produce stems and flowers that reach above the ground toward the light. A carpet of colorful flowers can suddenly cover the desert. These plants do not live long, so the flowers very quickly produce a lot of small, hard seeds. When the flowers die, the seeds fall and sink into the ground. They stay below the surface of the land until the next rains fall, when they will burst into life again.

These flowers have bloomed in California's Colorado Desert following heavy rains.

Get Smart!

Some desert flowering plants make seeds that can lie dormant in the ground for years, ready to burst into life when the rains finally come.

The pebble or living stone plant has a pair of fat leaves that are swollen with water. These look like stones, with a gap between them. These plants often grow together in clumps and look just like other rocks on the desert ground. This disguise helps the plants hide from desert animals that would like to eat the water-filled leaves. Once a year, each plant grows a single flower up from the space between the pair of leaves. Before it dies, the flower produces seeds that can grow into new plants.

Living stone plants are found in the deserts of southern Africa. The top part of each leaf contains a sunscreen to help protect the leaf from the scorching sun.

Get flowchart smart!

A Desert Flower Life Cycle

Let's take a look at a desert flower's life cycle.

When rain falls in the desert, some flowering plants immediately start to grow.

The seeds stay in the cool shade belowground until the next rains fall, when they will burst into life again.

Seeds that have been dormant beneath the surface start to grow stems and flowers. These reach above the ground toward the light.

A carpet of colorful flowers seems to suddenly cover the desert.

The plants do not live long, so the flowers quickly produce a lot of small, hard seeds.

When the flowers die, the seeds fall and sink into the ground.

Flowchart Smart

Chapter 3

Animal Adaptations

Adaptations are special behaviors, features, or body parts that living things develop over time to help them survive in an ecosystem. In deserts, animals must adapt to survive on little water and cope with extreme heat.

A behavioral adaptation is a way of behaving that helps a living thing survive in its ecosystem. The desert tortoise survives in burning hot deserts by keeping out of the heat in an underground burrow. The burrow can be up to 6 feet (2 m) deep. It also hides the tortoise from coyotes and other desert **predators**. If it is attacked when it leaves its burrow, the tortoise pulls its head, legs, and tail under its shell for protection.

Desert tortoises have shovel-like front feet with long, tough nails that are good for digging burrows and watering holes.

A physical adaptation is a body feature that helps an animal survive. Scorpions have four pairs of clawed legs that help them run quickly across hot desert sand. The huge pincers at the front of the body are used for digging burrows in which the scorpions can escape the heat in the daytime. The pincers are also used for grabbing and killing insects, spiders, and other **prey**. Scorpions sometimes use their pincers to hold prey still while they bring down their large, curved tail and sting it.

A scorpion's tough outer covering protects them from the hot sun and prevents them from losing too much water.

Get Smart!

Desert tortoises get most of the water they need to survive from the desert plants that they eat. They also dig shallow pits in the sand that collect water when it rains. The tortoises return to their watering holes to drink, then store water in their **bladder** so they can reabsorb it during a long dry spell.

On the Move

Traveling across hot deserts is hard. The sun heats the surface of the ground so much that it can be painful to touch. Animals' feet also sink easily into fine, soft sand, making it hard work to move forward.

Sidewinders are covered in rough scales that help them grip the sand as they move quickly across the hot desert.

Sidewinder snakes live in deserts where daytime temperatures are so hot that the sand could burn their skin if they dragged their entire 2.5-foot (76 cm) belly too slowly over the surface. To prevent this, they loop and raise their body into waves as they move, so that just two short sections of it touch the sand at any one time. When the sections touch the sand, they push against it, moving the snake sideways. When they stop moving, they quickly burrow under the surface to reach cooler sand or dive into a burrow for shade.

Camels have often been described as the ships of the desert. This is because they are the only animals that can carry people and goods across wide deserts. Camels' feet are well adapted for desert travel. They have large, thick footpads that are filled with fat to help them walk more easily over sand and stony ground. These feet are also extra wide to spread their weight over a bigger area. This keeps them from sinking into the sand as they trudge slowly along.

Camels have eyelashes that are 4 inches (10 cm) long. They keep sand from blowing into their eyes as they sit and rest or walk across the desert.

Get Smart!

Many people believe a camel's hump stores water, but this isn't true. Instead, camels store fat in their humps that can provide energy when food is scarce. Camels can survive long periods without water, but after a drought they can guzzle down enough water to fill a bathtub in just 10 minutes!

Amazing Adaptations

Some desert animals have some incredible adaptations to help them survive the challenges of living in a desert ecosystem.

The fennec fox is the smallest fox in the world. It measures only about 15 inches (38 cm) long, with an 8-inch (20 cm) tail. Its huge ears can be half the length of its body. Like many desert animals, fennec foxes keep out of the desert sun as much as they can because it is too hot. When they hunt, their huge ears help them hear prey moving around beneath the sand. Those big ears also help keep the foxes cool when they do venture out in daytime.

Get Smart!

A fennec fox keeps cool by releasing excess heat from its oversized ears. Its ears have more **blood vessels** per square inch than any other part of its body. These blood vessels lie just below the surface of the skin. As blood passes through them, heat from the blood escapes through the thin layer of skin and into the air. This cools the blood before it circulates back to the body, keeping the fox from overheating in the desert sun.

A fennec fox's ears are so sensitive that the fox can easily detect beetle, spider, and scorpion prey scuttling around the desert.

A thorny devil is a type of reptile that lives in hot deserts. It has an armor of spikes along its back to protect it from predators. The thorny devil also has an unusual way of getting the water it needs. When rain or dew lands on its back, the water flows along grooves in its body that lead to the corners of its mouth so that it can drink.

The thorny devil's spikes protect it from predators while it is busy hunting. This reptile can eat up to 3,000 ants each day in its desert home.

Get flowchart smart!

How Fennec Foxes Cool Off

Discover how a fennec fox's ears help keep it cool in a hot desert.

A fennec fox's ears have more blood vessels per square inch than any other part of its body.

This cools the blood before it circulates back to the body.

This prevents the fox from overheating in the desert sun.

These blood vessels lie just below the surface of the skin.

As blood passes through the vessels, heat from the blood escapes through the thin layer of skin and into the air.

Flowchart Smart

Chapter 4

Food Chains

All living things in an ecosystem need food to give them energy to grow, move, hunt, and survive. We can show the way energy flows from one living thing to another in a food chain.

Producers are living things that produce their own food. In desert food chains, plants are the producers. They are first in the food chain because they make their own food inside their bodies by the process of **photosynthesis**. Plants trap sunlight and use its energy to turn water and **carbon dioxide**, a gas in the air, into sugars and oxygen. Most plants trap sunlight in their leaves. Cacti do not have leaves because plants lose water through their leaves. Instead, they use their green stems to trap sunlight and photosynthesize.

Desert gerbils eat grasses and seeds, and some insects.

Animals that eat producers and one another are called **consumers**. In the desert, insects have hard, horny mouthparts to help them chew leaves. Birds, such as the cactus wren, feed on a sugary juice called nectar, which is found in the center of cactus flowers. Small desert rodents—such as kangaroo rats, jerboas, and gerbils—eat seeds. They often cram seeds into pouches in their cheeks. They carry the seeds into underground burrows where they store them to eat later when food is scarce.

Get Smart!

Desert hummingbirds are small birds that feed on nectar from desert flowers. They have long, pointed beaks for probing into the flowers for nectar. Their wings can flap at high speed to allow them to hover steadily in front of flowers while they feed.

Hummingbirds are named for the humming sound created by the rapid beating of their wings as they hover.

Desert Predators

Desert predators track, chase, and catch animals that eat plants, and they eat other predators, too. Desert predators are called secondary consumers because they come after the plant consumers in a food chain.

Desert chameleons are predators that hunt during the day. In the hottest part of the day, a chameleon can turn a lighter color to help keep cool while its pointed eyes move in different directions, looking out for prey. When it spots a beetle, its long legs and sand-colored body help it creep slowly closer to its victim. It then quickly shoots out its very long tongue at high speed. The prey is caught on the bulging, sticky tip at the end of the tongue. The tongue pulls back in, and the lizard swallows its dinner.

Desert rattlesnakes often rest in the shade during the day and hunt during the night, when many small animals come out of their burrows to feed. Rattlesnakes do not need light to see their prey. They can detect the heat that **warm-blooded** animals such as mice give off. Rattlesnakes are also known as pit vipers because they have a heat-sensing pit located behind each nostril on their head. This pit can detect very tiny differences in temperature, helping the snake locate and stalk its dinner.

In the Namib Desert, a sidewinder adder darts out from its hiding place just under the sand and kills a large lizard with its deadly **venom**.

This chameleon has caught a tok tokkie beetle on its sticky tongue, and pulled it quickly into its mouth.

Get Smart!

Coyotes are an apex, or top, predator in the Mojave Desert ecosystem. They eat desert tortoises that eat desert plants. They are at the top of the food chain because they eat other animals but are not killed and eaten by any other animal themselves.

Cheating Death

There are a lot of different food chains in a desert ecosystem. Some prey animals in food chains have defenses to try to avoid being eaten. But sometimes there is no escape from predators that have adapted to deal with these protections.

In the Kalahari Desert, termites build tall mounds of mud to shelter from the heat and eat desert plants, such as cacti. Scorpions use their powerful front pincers to grab and hold a termite still while they bring down their tail to inject venom into it. Meerkats have a long snout to sniff out scorpions in their burrows. They use their curved claws to dig up their prey. Meerkats quickly and carefully bite off and spit out the scorpion's stinger before eating it, to avoid getting stung themselves. Eagles eat meerkats by swooping down from above and snatching them away.

While some meerkats feed, other meerkats keep a lookout for predators and make a warning cry if one comes near.

The roadrunner is a desert bird that can run so fast that it can catch and eat fast-moving rattlesnakes. It is also one of the few desert animals that can eat snakes such as the copperhead, which injects venom through fangs in its mouth. The bird catches the snake by the tail, beats its head against the ground until it is dead, and then swallows it whole!

Get Smart!

Sometimes several different animals eat the same foods. Eagles and hawks hunt meerkats from the air. Jackals, wild cats, and snakes hunt meerkats on the ground. Many food chains linked together are called a **food web**.

Roadrunners not only eat snakes, they also eat insects, scorpions, lizards, rodents, and even other birds.

Get flowchart smart!

A Meerkat Food Chain

Let's follow the links in a meerkat food chain.

In the Kalahari Desert, termites eat desert plants such as cacti.

Eagles eat meerkats. The eagles swoop down from above and snatch the meerkats away.

Scorpions eat termites. They use their front pincers to grab and hold a termite still. Then they bring down their tail to inject venom into it to kill it, then eat it.

Meerkats eat scorpions. They have a long snout to sniff out scorpions in their burrows. They use their claws to dig up their prey.

Meerkats quickly and carefully bite off and spit out the stinger before eating the scorpion, to avoid being stung themselves.

Chapter 5

Desert Interactions

The different living and nonliving parts of a desert ecosystem are interconnected. They rely on each other to keep healthy and to survive.

Decomposers are animals that help break down waste and dead plants and animals. They play a vital role in the desert ecosystem. As they break down the remains of living things, they release **nutrients** from the waste and **recycle** them back into desert soils. This keeps desert soils healthy and helps plants, which form the basis of desert food chains, grow. Termites drag grass into their mounds, where it rots and breaks down. **Bacteria** also break down remains, absorbing, or soaking up, some of the nutrients to help them grow. The remainder of the nutrients sinks into the soil.

This huge termite mound is in the desert in western Australia. Termites chew up dying wood materials and plant remains, which helps them decompose faster.

Carrion beetles get some of their food from the remains of dead animals. Female carrion beetles also lay their eggs on animal remains. The larvae, or young, that hatch out of the eggs feed on the rotting corpse. This helps the larvae grow into adult beetles and it also helps break down the dead animal body. Without decomposers such as carrion beetles, the desert would soon be littered with dead animals and plants, and their nutrients would not be recycled to desert soils.

Get Smart!

Scarab beetles eat dung, or poop, of other desert animals and dead animals and plants. When they **digest** waste to obtain nutrients from the dung for themselves, they also release some nutrients back into the soil. They dig tunnel-like nests in the ground and fill them with dung for their larvae to feed on.

A scarab beetle rolls its ball of dung away from the dung pile to keep other beetles from stealing it.

Help at Hand

The living things in an ecosystem are not just interconnected by being part of the same food chain or web. In a desert, plants and animals also rely on each other in different ways.

Why do some desert plants use some of their energy to make fruits? The tasty fruits attract hungry animals to eat them. This helps the animals. But the animals also swallow the seeds inside the fruit and later spit them out or release them inside their dung, often in the shade of another plant or burrow. These damp, shady spots are ideal places for seeds to grow into new plants.

Birds do not only use cactus plants for food. The Gila woodpecker has a very strong head and strong neck muscles. This helps it use its hard, pointed beak to peck out holes inside a saguaro cactus. It then uses the hole as a nest in which to lay its eggs. This helps other birds, too. When a woodpecker abandons a hole after its chicks have flown the nest, elf owls, screech owls, finches, or sparrows may move in.

Javelinas eat fruit from the prickly pear cactus and the pads from which the fruit grows, which are an extremely important source of water.

The inside of a saguaro cactus provides a safe, cool place for Gila woodpeckers to raise their young.

Get Smart!

A javelina is a wild, pig-like animal. It eats prickly pear fruits in the deserts of Mexico and the southwestern United States. Its poop can be full of seeds from the fruits. This acts as a natural fertilizer to help the seeds grow into new prickly pear plants in new locations. Much of Texas's landscape is covered with patches of cactus, probably distributed by javelina poop!

Sharing the Space

Animals that share the same space in an ecosystem often have some surprising ways of helping one another or working together to ensure that they can both survive.

Animals that hunt for the same animals in a desert ecosystem may exist in different niches. A niche is a living thing's role in an ecosystem. For example, hawks, eagles, and falcons hunt for small animals such as lizards and rodents during the day. Owls hunt for the same or similar creatures at night. Vultures swoop down from on high and **scavenge**. Having different niches means these animals can eat similar foods without directly competing with one another.

Harris hawks hunt prey such as small mammals, birds, and lizards. Sometimes two or more Harris hawks work as a team to hunt prey.

Some animals are so interconnected that they are known as keystone species. Coyotes are a keystone species because they have such a big impact on their ecosystem. Coyotes keep a check on the number of smaller predators by eating them, which allows prey of those smaller predators to survive. For example, small desert predators eat the eggs and chicks of birds that nest on the ground. If there were no coyotes, there would be more small predators, and that would mean there would be far fewer birds.

Coyotes help keep the jackrabbit population under control, which helps keep the desert ecosystem healthy.

Get Smart!

Coyotes eat sage grouse, but having coyotes around also helps these birds. Coyotes hunt and eat jackrabbits. This limits the number of eagles that feed on sage grouse eggs and chicks because jackrabbits are an important source of food for the eagles. Jackrabbits also eat plants that sage grouse eat. With fewer jackrabbits, there is less competition for food for the sage grouse.

Get flowchart smart!

How Carrion Beetles Clean Deserts

Let's learn how carrion beetles help keep desert ecosystems healthy.

Carrion beetles get some of their food from the remains of dead animals. Female carrion beetles also lay their eggs on animal remains.

Without decomposers such as carrion beetles, the desert would soon be littered with dead animals and plants, and their nutrients would not be recycled to desert soils.

The larvae that hatch out of the eggs feed on the rotting corpse.

This allows the larvae to grow into adult beetles, and it also helps break down the dead animal's body.

Flowchart Smart

Chapter 6

The Future for Desert Ecosystems

A desert ecosystem exists in a delicate balance. Because the nonliving and living parts in that ecosystem are interconnected, changing one part can put the entire ecosystem out of balance and under threat.

Some desert ecosystems are threatened by **habitat** destruction. This happens in different ways. People take over desert land to build towns. As well as taking land, people also pump up water from below desert soils to use themselves, reducing the water available for plants and animals. People also dig deep mines to extract oil or gas. The waste from this can **pollute** the land nearby. Another major problem is overgrazing. This is when herds of goats or other farm animals graze on the edges of deserts and eat too many desert plants. This can destroy vital producers in the desert food chain.

The city of Dubai lies directly within the Arabian Desert. Building offices and highways destroys the natural habitat.

Overgrazing is affecting desert tortoises. In some parts of the Mojave Desert, in the United States, overgrazing by farm animals such as sheep, cattle, and wild burros has destroyed food plants that are important to desert tortoises. Heavy farm animals also stamp down the ground so heavily that it becomes harder and compacted. It is then less able to absorb rainwater. Plants do not grow well in ground like this. Cattle and sheep also compete with the tortoises for sparse food plants in the area and can damage the entrances to the desert tortoises' burrows.

When tourists and other visitors to desert ecosystems drive offroad, they can crush plants and scare away wildlife.

Get Smart!

When plants die due to overgrazing, the soil is affected. Plant roots hold the top fertile layer of soil together. When the plants have gone, any fertile soil is blown away, leaving only dusty land on which very little can grow.

Get flowchart smart!

Overgrazing and Desert Tortoises

Discover how overgrazing affects desert tortoises.

In some parts of the Mojave Desert, overgrazing by farm animals such as sheep, cattle, and wild burros has destroyed plants that are important to desert tortoises.

With less food to eat and fewer burrows to escape into, desert tortoise numbers have fallen.

Heavy farm animals stamp down the ground so heavily that it becomes compacted and less able to absorb rainwater. Plants struggle to grow there.

Cattle and sheep also damage entrances to the desert tortoises' burrows.

Flowchart Smart

Protecting Desert Ecosystems

Deserts are among the most fragile and threatened ecosystems on Earth. So, what is being done to help them and all their amazing plants and animals?

Scientists study desert ecosystems in order to better understand them. This can help them figure out what can damage desert ecosystems and how best to help them. They may, for example, recommend which plants to grow in an area of desert that has been overgrazed, and when to plant them. Scientists also study the impact of **invasive** species. These are plants or animals that are not **native** to the area and may destroy local wildlife. Volunteers can then focus on removing the invasive species that most threaten native plants and animals in the desert.

In desert **conservation** areas, people are not allowed to build on, dig mines in, take water from, or otherwise damage the ecosystem in any way.

Conservation organizations protect ecosystems such as deserts. They raise awareness of the importance of deserts and why people should help protect them. Conservation organizations also raise money to help protect **endangered** desert animals and to pay for national parks and other protected conservation areas that include deserts. Deserts are an important ecosystem and we should do all we can to help them have a healthy future.

Get Smart!

Buffelgrass is an invasive species that is affecting the Sonoran Desert. It is a very tall grass with windblown seeds that spread over wide areas, robbing native grasses of places to grow. It becomes very dry in summer, catches fire easily, and burns quickly. This can lead to destructive wildfires that burn native plants, too. The only way to destroy it is to remove it by hand.

Scientists are working on ways to help deserts. These scientists are researching levels of moisture in the Chilean desert air.

Glossary

adaptations Changes to suit a new situation.

arid Very dry.

bacteria Tiny living things that can help decompose waste.

bladder Part of an animal's body that stores urine.

blood vessels Tubes that carry blood around the body.

carbon dioxide A gas in the air.

climates The general weather that happens in regions over many years.

condenses Cools and turns from a gas into a liquid.

conservation The act of guarding, protecting, or preserving something.

consumers Animals that eat plants or other animals.

decomposers Living things that break down waste.

digest Break down so the body can use it.

ecosystems The living and nonliving things in places, interacting with one another.

endangered In danger of dying out.

evaporate Turn from a liquid into a gas.

food web The feeding relationships between food chains in an ecosystem.

habitat The natural environment of a living thing.

interact Act in such a way as to have an effect on one another.

invasive A living thing that is new to an area and spreads, causing harm.

native Describes something that originates, or comes, from an area.

nutrients Substances that living things need to survive and grow.

photosynthesis The process by which green plants make sugary food using the energy in sunlight.

poles The two points at opposite ends of Earth, the North Pole and South Pole.

pollute To put something into water, air, or land that damages it or makes it harmful to living things.

precipitation Water that falls from clouds, especially as rain or snow.

predators Animals that catch and eat other animals.

prey An animal hunted and eaten by another animal.

producers Living things that make their own food inside their body.

recycle Convert waste into something new.

scavenge Find and feed on dead animals or waste.

venom Poison.

warm-blooded An animal that makes its own warmth.

water vapor The gas form of water.

For More Information

Books

Barghoorn, Linda. *Map and Track Deserts* (Map and Track Biomes and Animals). New York, NY: Crabtree Publishing Company, 2019.

Newland, Sonya. *Atacama Desert Research Journal* (Ecosystems Research Journal). New York, NY: Crabtree Publishing Company, 2018.

Patkau, Karen. *Who Needs a Desert?* (Ecosystem Series). Toronto, ON: Tundra Books, 2014.

Wolny, Philip. *What Are Deserts?* (Let's Find Out! Biomes). New York, NY: Rosen Publishing, 2019.

Websites

Take a mission to the desert at this website:
https://earthobservatory.nasa.gov/experiments/biome/biodesert.php

For details on desert locations, plants, animals, and weather, visit:
http://kids.nceas.ucsb.edu/biomes/desert.html

Learn more about deserts at:
www.nationalgeographic.com/environment/habitats/deserts

Find more facts about the desert biome at:
https://ucmp.berkeley.edu/glossary/gloss5/biome/deserts.html

Publisher's note to educators and parents: Our editors have carefully reviewed these websites to ensure that they are suitable for students. Many websites change frequently, however, and we cannot guarantee that a site's future contents will continue to meet our high standards of quality and educational value. Be advised that students should be closely supervised whenever they access the Internet.

Index